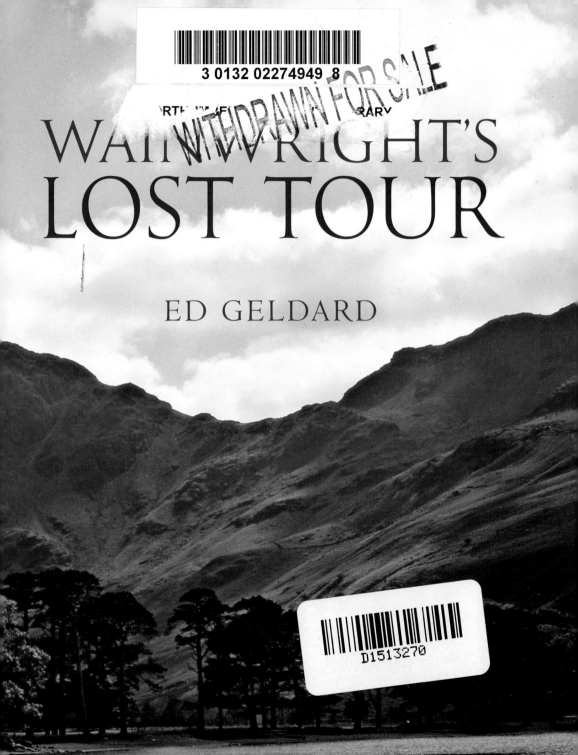

WAINWRIGHT'S
LOST TOUR

ED GELDARD

AMBERLEY

FOR A.W.

'And in the darkest hours of urban depression,
I will sometimes take out that dog's eared map
And dream awhile of more spacious days and
perhaps a dried blade of grass will fall out of it
to remind me that I was once a freeman on the hills.'

H. Sidgewick
Cockley Beck Farm sitting room
July 1924

This edition first published 2013

Amberley Publishing
The Hill, Stroud,
Gloucestershire, GL5 4EP
www.amberley-books.com

Photographs & Text © Ed Geldard, 2010, 2013

The right of Ed Geldard to be identified as the
Author of this work has been asserted in accordance with
the Copyrights, Designs and Patents Act 1988.

ISBN 978 1 4456 1435 9

British Library Cataloguing in Publication Data.
A catalogue record for this book is available from the
British Library.

Typesetting by Amberley Publishing.
Printed in Great Britain.

CONTENTS

ACKNOWLEDGEMENTS

I would like to acknowledge the help given by Joan Self of the National Meteorological Archive; it was she who, time and again, answered all my queries about the weather at the time of the Tour. Thank you Joan.

My thanks also go to LD Mountain Centre for supplying the clothing and rucksacks; to Don Bennett of Durham for scanning the transparencies; to Frances Lincoln, holders of the Wainwright rights; to Gary Craven who rebuilt my old computer at the most critical point; to Jasper Hadman of Amberley Publishing for his meticulous editing; to Cedric Iley for re-checking the map references for me; and to Jocelin Winthrop-Young for permission to use his father's poem.

All played their part in making this book what it is. Any errors, which I'm sure you will find, are mine and mine alone.

Of all of those who helped me, the greatest debt I owe is to Mag. Over the course of the eight months that I spent on the tour, her commitment and enthusiasm outstripped my own. Without her help none of the images in this book would have been taken.

THE AUTHOR

Ed Geldard is a professional landscape photographer, who, after a short spell in the Lake District, has now returned to live in his native North East. A former freelancer for the *Northern Echo* Group, he is a keen walker and contributes to many countryside publications. In 1991 he teamed up with the legendary Alfred Wainwright who said that his beautiful pictures 'speak louder than words'. *The Sunday Times* labelled them as 'stunningly magnificent'.

Together they produced *Wainwright in the Limestone Dales* which became an overnight best seller. Commissioned in 1992 for *Wainwright's Tour in the Lake District*, winner of the Tullie House prize in the 'Lakeland Book of the Year Award', he later went on to complete his own books *Travels through the Lakes, Northumberland & the Land of the Prince Bishops* and *Northumberland Strongholds*.

Author Photo: © Cedric Iley

INTRODUCTION

Yorkshire Dales 1989.

Outside rain beat incessantly against the window; McCaskill had got it wrong again. Inside the condensation ran in rivulets down the panes; scones, jam and cream long since gone. Approaching Garsdale Head we had taken a side road leading to Grisedale, sometimes referred to as 'the valley that died', then on again past The Moor Cock Inn and Aisgill before stopping in the village of Nateby. Here, in the warmth of a small tearoom, events that would change my outlook and opinion forever were about to take place. The cigarette, which had now replaced the familiar pipe of my companion, looked strangely out of place. 'Do you want to do the book?' he asked in a matter-of-fact way. For a moment I sat quite still, not sure if I had heard correctly. 'What does it involve?' I replied. His eyes twinkled with enthusiasm. 'Fifteen chapters, 213 pages, and 230 photographs. From Kendal in the West to Wharfedale in the East, from Keld in the North to Malham in the South ... Limestone Country.'

From the high ground I gazed down at the Buttertubs through a cold heavy drizzle; I was there because Alfred Wainwright had asked, 'Is it possible to take a photogenic shot to show all five pots?' Mentally I had begun to question the reason for this unasked-for outing and introduction to Alfred Wainwright. The reason had now become quite clear. The *Westmorland Gazette* was to publish his next book, and Wainwright was offering me the photography.

We had met for the first time some two hours earlier, when Andrew Nichol, the editor of the *Westmorland Gazette*, had popped into the studio and asked me if I had a couple of hours to spare to go for a drive. 'I want you to meet someone,' he said. A meeting with Alfred Wainwright was the last thing I imagined. It was the beginning of a friendship that lasted until his death.

The Lake District is a unique panorama of mountains, valleys and lakes, unequalled anywhere in the country. Each mile opens up fresh and wonderful views. Roads that wind through green and narrow valleys lead, after a few miles, to steep impressive passes, frowned on by soaring Gothic crags.

The lakes themselves differ one from another, not only in size and shape, but also in surroundings, character and atmosphere; never the same from one day to the next, nor, more obviously, from one month or season to the next. Different weather, different cloud formation, different colouring and light: there is always something new. On the subject of rain, many will say, 'Doesn't it always rain in the Lake District?' Well, it has been said that Seathwaite in Borrowdale remains indelibly marked as the wettest place in England, with 130 inches of rain a year (although local rumour has it that this is simply down to Borrowdale Mountain Rescue Team relieving themselves into the rain gauge after a hard day on the fells!). The answer is that it doesn't. It is a common factor in all mountain areas that, generally, when it rains it rains hard, but quite often it will clear unbelievably quickly. It must be remembered too that if there was not any rain, there would be no becks tumbling down the fellsides, and no lakes into which they could tumble.

It was in 1930 that Alfred Wainwright made his first visit to the Lake District. So taken was he by the beauty of the fells that when he returned home to the mill town of Blackburn he began to make plans for the following year, for he was determined to see everything worth seeing. On Saturday, 23 May 1931, he and his three companions set out on their spring holiday; who would have believed it would turn out to be such a test of endurance.

In 1993 Michael Joseph published *Wainwright's Tour in the Lake District – Whitsuntide 1931* as part of their Wainwright series. Eric Maudsley tells us in his introduction that a number of variations were made to the walk. In the Sources and Acknowledgements section of the book we are informed that the walk lasted for seven days rather than six; Jenny Dereham tells us that this information came from the introduction by Eric Maudsley. After reading it through several times I can find no reference to an extra day, only slight variations to the first four days.

Wainwright accepted that because of the late arrival at Windermere an alternative route was required on the first day, but not on the days that were to follow. The tour was conceived to see every mountain, lake and valley in the Lake District within the space of six days.

The conclusions that I have come to regarding these variations are drawn from a lifetime's experience on the fells.

DAY 1

23 May 1931, Windermere to Patterdale

Weather forecast: *Cloudy with some lightning, heavy rain in evening.*

Eric Maudsley informs us in his introduction that it was early evening as they approached Ill Bell. He also tells us that the party retreated to the Troutbeck area to seek accommodation for the night. Wainwright's timetable puts this around 7 p.m.

It is my theory that, because of the heavy rain, the group retraced their steps to Yoke and then descended into Troutbeck Park. My reasoning is that if they had left Ill Bell they were committed to continuing the ridge as far as Thornthwaite, from where they could have dropped down to Threshthwaite Mouth and Hartsop. This, however, would mean another two hours in the driving rain. The following day the small party would have probably made the short journey via the Kirkstone Pass to Patterdale to start day two.

DAY 2

24 May 1931, Patterdale to Keswick

Weather forecast: *Very cloudy with rain at times.*

Maudsley tells us that they had to leave out Blencathra on day two. Again, in my opinion, this was due to the weather; although not as heavy, this was their second day of discomfort. We have no information as to where they left the route, but I believe it would have been at Sticks Pass or Calfhow Pike. From there, after descending to the road, it is but a short bus ride into Keswick.

DAY 3

25 May 1931, Keswick to Buttermere

Weather Forecast: *A cloudy morning followed by showers in the afternoon.*

Maudsley informs us that on day three Grasmoor was omitted from the schedule.

Wainwright's schedule tells us that they would have reached Dale Head just after noon. The morning had been cloudy and they were once again suffering from intermittent showers. Upon reaching Robinson around 3 p.m. they must have dropped down to Buttermere. This was because once they had crossed the road at Newlands they would be committed to Grasmoor and a further six hours of showers.

DAY 4

26 May 1931, Buttermere to Wasdale

Weather forecast: *Bright all day.*

Once again, we are told of a variation – the exclusion of Pillar.

This is the hardest day in the tour and I'm not surprised that they cut short their day. It was bright and hot for the time of year. I believe that on reaching the Black Sail Pass they made up their minds to descend into Wasdale. They would have been tired at this point, and again, this is the only escape route before being committed to the Pillar group.

DAY 5

27 May 1931, Wasdale to Langdale

Weather forecast: *Bright in the morning and afternoon turning to thunder and overcast in the evening.*
The second of the two good days, this time without any variations, but it was still a hard day with over 5,000 feet of ascent.

DAY 6

28 May 1931, Langdale to Windermere

Weather forecast: *Cloudy and overcast all day. Rain by evening.*
Again there are no variations that we know of. Wainwright's schedule tells us that it would have been around 5 p.m. when they reached Ambleside to start the long journey home by bus.

Whatever the reasons were, I have said enough and this is Wainwright's walk; go and see for yourselves, I am sure you will not regret it.

Ed Geldard

Note: For the technophiles, I used four cameras and a variety of lenses during this walk; these were a Hasselblad SWC, a 500C, a Bronica ETRSi and a Pentax MX. All images were in the pre-digital age. The film was Kodak EPP.

Throughout this walk I was following the footsteps of A.W.; using the six foolscap sheets that Eric Maudsley kept for six decades. I did not use the variations made to it by Michael Joseph in *Wainwright's Tour in the Lake District – Whitsuntide 1931*; in fact, it wasn't until the book was published that I learned of them. As I have said already, this was A.W.'s walk.

A.W. 1991.

PROLOGUE

Winter 1931.

Outside, the snow lay 2 feet deep in places. In the warmth of the Borough treasurer's office at Blackburn, the young man's eyes quickly scanned the sheets that lay on his desk. The work, done in his spare time, had taken him months of meticulous planning before it could be condensed into six foolscap sheets; the notes, such as they were, were made using a half inch Bartholomew's map of Westmorland and Cumberland. It was the outline of a proposed walking tour in the Lake District for the forthcoming Whitsuntide holiday of that year; he, with three of his colleagues, Jim Sharples, Harry Driver and Eric Maudsley, would embark on an adventure, dreamed of in the long winter months.

The previous year, at the age of twenty-three, Alfred Wainwright had taken his first holiday in the Lake District. Leaving behind his dreary life in the mill town, he found himself in a world of unbelievable beauty; the experience was 'a revelation so unexpected that I stood transfixed, unable to believe my eyes ... those few hours on Orrest Head cast a spell that changed my life.' On his return, he began to make his plans. The 'Tour' was to be the most comprehensive walk tackled to date. It was the year before his marriage to Ruth Holden; a marriage he was to regret over the next thirty-six years.

With Whitsuntide fast approaching, Wainwright addressed the small band in the warmth of his office. He told them that, with their time limit, it would be impossible to visit every corner of Lakeland; yet, if the route was painstakingly followed, the party would visit 'everywhere worth mentioning'. It would be arduous, but the rewards would be well worth the time and effort expended. It would avoid the tourist traps and picnic spots; its aim was to see every lake, every valley and every mountain in the District.

It would be 'THE GRAND TOUR'.

It was not until Alfred Wainwright's death, six decades later, that those six foolscap sheets once again saw the light of day.

Dun Bull Inn,
Mardale 1931.

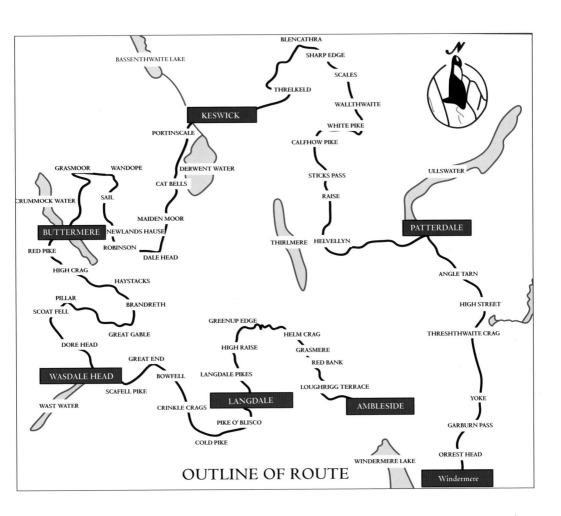

OUTLINE OF ROUTE

Day	From	To	A.W.'s Mileage	Approx. Mileage	Approx. Ascent in Ft.	A.W.'s Ascent
Saturday	Windermere	Patterdale	16	13.5	3,746	3,850
Sunday	Patterdale	Keswick	20	20.25	5,428	6,900
Monday	Keswick	Buttermere	19	18.25	6,455	6,650
Tuesday	Buttermere	Wasdale	18	16	6,485	7,750
Wednesday	Wasdale	Langdale	14.5	13.5	5,236	6,300
Thursday	Langdale	Windermere	15	15.5	3,049	3,400
		Totals	102.5	97	26,653	34,850

Note: All distances and ascents are approximate and should only be used as a guide.

* Naismith's Rule: Allow one hour for every 3 miles forward, and half an hour for every 1,000 feet of ascent.

A study by Leeds University in 1998 found it accurate within 25 per cent on routes in the Lake District.

DAY ONE
SATURDAY
23 May 1931

WINDERMERE TO PATTERDALE

Forecast: *Cloudy with some lightning, heavy rain in evening.*

From	To	Map ref.	Height	Mileage	Ascent	Descent
Windermere	Orrest Head	NY 4140 9937	783	0.5	383	0
Orrest Head	Dubbs Reservoir	NY 4220 0170	741	2	186	-204
Dubbs Reservoir	Garburn Pass	NY 4345 0445	1,480	2	739	0
Garburn Pass	Yoke	NY 4375 0675	2,316	1.5	836	0
Yoke	Ill Bell	NY 4370 0770	2,484	0.5	338	-170
Ill Bell	Froswick	NY 4350 0850	2,362	0.5	157	-280
Froswick	Thornthwaite Crag	NY 4300 1010	2,572	1	476	-266
Thornthwaite Crag	High Street	NY 4410 1110	2,719	1	249	-102
High Street	The Knott	NY 4370 1265	2,423	1.1	94	-390
The Knott	Angle Tarn	NY 4170 1440	1,572	1.5	0	-851
Angle Tarn	Angle Tarn Pikes	NY 4145 1470	1,860	0.3	288	0
Angle Tarn Pikes	Patterdale	NY 3900 1595	495	1.6	0	-1,365
	Totals for day			13.5	3,746	-3,628

ORREST HEAD

'The best time to visit the Lake District is between 1st of January and the 31st December', so said Christopher North. Windermere, or Winandermere as Wordsworth and other Lake poets called it, is the largest of the lakes. It derives its name from the Norse hero Winander or Vinandr.

From Orrest Head the lake gives an impression of its true size; a full 10 miles in length, it exhibits the most magnificent backdrop of mountains, not only in Westmorland but also in the whole world.

At the south end of the lake we have Coniston Old Man, and in the same direction Black Comb appears over Claife Heights, followed by Wetherlam, Wrynose Pass, Crinkle Crags, Scafell, Bowfell, Great Gable, Langdale Pikes, Loughrigg, Fairfield, Red Screes, Caudale Moor, Thornthwaite and many more in between. During the winter of 1896/97, when the lake was covered with thick ice, the railway company of the day ran excursions for skaters from London for six shillings (thirty pence) return.

DUBBS RESERVOIR
Anglers enjoying a quiet afternoon at Dubbs Reservoir.

TROUTBECK, SUMMER

The beautiful valley of Troutbeck was once a forest area, where harassed and terrified Brigantes took refuge from the Romans who were making their great road over High Street. Traces of an ancient settlement have been found on Troutbeck Tongue, the impudent elongated hill that divides the valley into two. Centuries later, the valley was enclosed and divided among the inhabitants.

TROUTBECK, WINTER

The snow-clad sentinels of Yoke, Ill Bell and Thornthwaite dominate Troutbeck Park, originally a medieval deer park belonging to the barons of Kendal. Beatrix Potter owned a farm here where she bred Herdwick sheep.

GARBURN PASS

Formerly an important packhorse route, this steep and stony track, known as the Garburn Pass, rises across the shoulder of Applethwaite Common. It is the only direct link between the valleys of Troutbeck and Kentmere. The long ascent, enclosed in part between low stone walls, allows arresting views of Yoke, Ill Bell, Froswick, Thornthwaite and Caudale moor. The upper valley is divided into two by Troutbeck Tongue.

YOKE SUMMIT

Yoke provides a gentle introduction to the ridge that runs north to Thornthwaite Beacon and High Street. From its summit we look to Ill Bell and Froswick.

13

RAINSBORROW CRAG

Kentmere, the source of the Kent, a river that gave its name to Kendal, is divided into two distinct areas. The lower part, now that it no longer has the mere, which for over a mile occupied the fields south of the church, is featureless. The upper valley is more characteristic, having the High Street range at its head. Above the disused quarries, the black precipice of Rainsborrow Crag rises above upper Kentmere.

KENTMERE VALLEY

The Kentmere Valley offers the fell walker not only a horseshoe ridge walk, but also the longest single high level ridge walk: from Sour Howes above Windermere to Arthur's Pike on the edge of Ullswater. The summit of Ill Bell gives a wonderful view of the valley.

ILL BELL SUMMIT

Ill Bell is usually climbed by way of the Garburn Pass from Troutbeck and along the ridge over Yoke. It is the highest and shapeliest of the peaks on this ridge leading to Thornthwaite Crag. The multiplicity of cairns that crowd the small top make it one of the most distinctive summits in Lakeland.

FROSWICK FROM ILL BELL

The ridge from Ill Bell to Thornthwaite Crag is a series of ups and downs. On the ridge ahead lies Thornthwaite Beacon and High Street.

Above: SCOTS RAKE
Wild fell ponies on Scots Rake, where in the distant past the marauding Scots swept along until they were cut down by Hugh Hird and his trusty longbow. In the distance we can see Froswick, Ill Bell and the Kentmere Valley.

Left: THORNTHWAITE BEACON
Thornthwaite Crag, topped by its 14-foot-high beacon, is the most distinctive summit in Lakeland, a landmark for miles around. This monolithic cairn stands west of the Roman road leading on to High Street, at an angle in the wall crossing the summit. The most scenic route to the beacon is by way of Yoke, Ill Bell and Froswick, from the Garburn Pass.

HIGH STREET

High Street and its satellites make an ideal ridge walking area. The flat crest that carries the Roman road is seen here from Thornthwaite Beacon.

HIGH STREET SUMMIT

The summit trig point of High Street could stand almost anywhere on this flat featureless plateau, and it's no wonder that the people from the valleys used to hold horse races up here. From the summit we look across to Great Gable and the Scafell range.

RACECOURSE HILL, HIGH STREET

High Street takes its name from the Roman road (the 'Street'), which traverses the fellside linking 'GALAVA', near Ambleside, to 'BROVACUM', near Penrith. The summit, marked by an Ordnance Survey column, is a vast grassy plateau with a tumbledown wall running north to south over the crest, where, until 1835, an annual shepherds' meet took place with wrestling and horse racing.

The horse racing and sport finally came to an end, and were merged into the Shepherds' meet at Mardale. A pleasant way to climb High Street from the west is to start at Low Hartsop and walk up Pasture Beck.

HIGH STREET DESCENT

The grassy promenade of the High Street ridge descends to a narrow depression at the Straits of Riggindale before climbing again towards the Knott. This is the most popular ridge walk of the eastern fells.

MARDALE

Mardale was once described as 'a hamlet, unforgettable for the charm of its romantic beauty and seclusion from the world'. This was before 1919 when Manchester Corporation acquired Haweswater Lake in Mardale, together with 24,000 acres of surrounding catchment area, for its conversion into a reservoir. The water level was raised by almost a hundred feet and the tiny village of Mardale disappeared. During the summer drought of 1995, the reservoir was drawn down further than it had been since its construction in 1936. As the weeks passed, the waters continued to recede and the remains of the drowned hamlet slowly re-emerged from beneath the lake. From our viewpoint we look over Goosemire to Chapel Bridge and into Riggingdale. The Knott is of little interest and is only a small cairn on a grassy mound, easily reached along the High Street ridge.

ANGLE TARN

'The mountain tarns,' said Wordsworth, 'can only be recommended to the notice of the inquisitive traveller who has time to spare.'

On a sunny day, Angle Tarn is a favourite place for picnics and is easily reached from Patterdale via the Boardale path. This beautiful sheet of water, with its islands and calm, clear waters, is passed on the descent from High Street and makes a perfect foreground for the distant Helvellyn range.

ANGLE TARN PIKES

From the northern Pike of Angle tarn we look across Deepdale to Helvellyn and St Sunday Crag. At one time Deepdale was thought by many to be the most important centre in the eastern fells.

DESCENT INTO PATTERDALE

On the descent from Boardale Hause, walkers may pause a moment and enjoy the view of Patterdale and the surrounding fells.

NOTE

Wainwright tells us that it would not be possible for the party to leave Windermere until late afternoon, and therefore some diversion of the route would be required. He suggests two alternatives:

(1) From Thornthwaite Crag they could descend via Threshthwaite Cove to Low Hartsop, and from there make for Patterdale. This would amend the figures to read five and a half hours of travel, 14 miles and 3,100 feet of ascent.

(2) From the Windermere Reservoir they could follow the valley alongside the River Trout to Troutbeck Park, skirt round The Tongue and climb up to Threshthwaite Cove before descending to Patterdale via Pasture Beck. This would reduce the climbing to a minimum and, other than going via the Kirkstone Pass, it is the shortest practical route to Patterdale. The revised timings for this would be four to four and a half hours of travel, 12 miles and 2,050 feet of ascent.

Because of inclement weather conditions the party were forced into a third option: they had to descend to the Troutbeck area and seek accommodation for the night.

THRESHTHWAITE MOUTH

From the eastern edge of Thornthwaite Crag one looks down into Threshthwaite Cove. The desolate walls of the Cove rise up to form the col between the steep shale slopes of Thornthwaite Crag and the rugged slopes of Caudale Moor. This is Threshthwaite Mouth.

HARTSOP

Nestling in a secluded valley a few miles from Patterdale, the tiny hamlet of Hartsop contains several interesting seventeenth-century buildings and cottages with spinning galleries. In the days of William Rufus the area around Hartsop was a hunting forest, and it takes its name from the deer that ran here. In winter, deer from the Martindale herd can sometimes be seen on Hartsop and Caudale Moor.

THE KIRKSTONE

Below Red Screes, among the fallen boulders only a few yards from the roadside, is the boulder that gives the pass its name, the Kirkstone. On the long ascent from Ullswater, its silhouette, said to resemble a kirk, is conspicuous on the skyline. Wordsworth says:

> *This block — and yon, whose church-like frame*
> *Gives to this savage pass its name*

DAY TWO
SUNDAY
24 May 1931

PATTERDALE TO KESWICK

Forecast: *Very cloudy with rain at times.*

From	To	Map ref.	Height	Mileage	Ascent	Descent
Patterdale	Grassthwaitehowe	NY 3850 1595	850	1.5	355	0
Grassthwaitehowe	Striding Edge	NY 3485 1495	2,687	2	1,837	0
Striding Edge	Helvellyn	NY 3415 1512	3,113	0.5	426	0
Helvellyn	Helvellyn Low Man	NY 3370 1550	3,033	0.5	84	-164
Helvellyn Low Man	Raise	NY 3435 1745	2,889	1.25	144	-419
Raise	Sticks Pass	NY 3420 1820	2,457	0.5	0	-432
Sticks Pass	Stybarrow Dod	NY 3444 1884	2,690	0.5	233	0
Stybarrow Dod	Watson Dod	NY 3355 1955	2,584	0.5	0	-106
Watson Dod	Great Dod	NY 3425 2045	2,807	0.75	223	0
Great Dod	Calfhow Pike	NY 3305 2112	2,166	1	0	-641
Calfhow Pike	White Pike	NY 3375 2297	2,105	1.25	0	-61
White Pike	Wallthwaite	NY 3540 2620	558	4.25	0	-1,547
Wallthwaite	Scales	NY 3430 2690	781	1	223	-20
Scales	Sharp Edge	NY 3275 2835	2,254	1.5	1,473	0
Sharp Edge	Blencathra	NY 3240 2805	2,848	0.75	430	0
Blencathra	Threlkeld	NY 3220 2540	528	2.5	0	-2,320
	Totals for day			20.25	5,428	-5,710

Bus to Keswick

PATTERDALE

Mountains are the natural boundaries of Patterdale or Patrick's Dale, the small hamlet situated at the head of Ullswater. Tradition says that in AD 504 St Patrick passed through the dale performing baptisms at a holy well that is still preserved by the roadside. Today's visitor passes over the same well-trodden routes to High Street and Kidsey Pike; others may go by way of the old packhorse trails to Howtown on the eastern side of Ullswater, or through Grisedale to Helvellyn.

From St Sunday Crag we look down on Ullswater, Patterdale and Grassthwaitehow.

HELVELLYN AND CATSTYCAM

In Victorian times, the tourist rode from Patterdale up a pony track by way of Kepple Cove and on to Red Tarn. There they would tether their animals before ascending the slopes of Catstycam and Swirrel Edge to the summit of Helvellyn. Seen from Birkhouse Moor, the sombre, precipitous east face of Helvellyn contrasts sharply with the smooth flanks of Catstycam.

STRIDING EDGE

With sheer fellside on either side, the mile-long arête of Striding Edge is the most frequented and exciting ridge scramble to the summit of Helvellyn. It was here, on what De Quincy called the 'awful curtain of rock', that Charles Gough was killed in 1805. Combined with the descent of Swirrel Edge, the traverse of Helvellyn by Striding Edge has become a Lake District classic.

Above: STRIDING EDGE AND RED TARN

The panorama from the summit of Helvellyn is striking. On a clear day almost every fell in Lakeland can be seen. Almost 1,000 feet below, nestling between the two long arms of Striding Edge and Swirrel Edge, is Red Tarn, whose round contours contrast with the narrow arête of Striding Edge, and the gentle slopes of Birkhouse Moor.

Left: GOUGH MEMORIAL

This large memorial standing above Striding Edge, close to the summit plateau of Helvellyn, records the death of Charles Gough, a Manchester artist who, in the spring of 1805, fell to his death while attempting to cross from Patterdale to Wythburn. The story of his faithful dog, which accompanied him and remained watching his body for three months after that fateful day, has been immortalised by Scott and Wordsworth.

The dog, which still was hovering nigh,
Repeating the same cry,
This dog, had been through three months' space
A dweller in that savage place.

HELVELLYN SUMMIT

A mountain's popularity does not always equate to the size of its summit cairn. Helvellyn, third highest in the Lake District, is visited almost every day of the year, yet only a small, insignificant pyramid of stones marks the plateau summit. A short distance away, a small stone memorial tablet commemorates the landing of an aeroplane, piloted by Bert Hindle and John Leeming, on the mountain plateau on 22 December 1926.

ST SUNDAY FROM HELVELLYN

From Helvellyn we look across Striding Edge to the shapely ridge of St Sunday Crag, with its steep scree and rocky buttress falling away northward into Grisedale. Because of the close proximity of Fairfield and Helvellyn, it is doubtful whether it is ever ascended for itself alone.

SWIRRAL EDGE
Two ridges lead to the summit of Helvellyn: Striding Edge and Swirral Edge. Combining both with the ascent of Helvellyn makes a classic traverse.

HELVELLYN LOWER MAN
A short distance from the summit of Helvellyn lies Helvellyn Lower Man. From here there is a discernible fall before a rise over the next half mile to White Side.

THIRLMERE

Mid-way between Ambleside and Keswick, in the shadows of Helvellyn, lies Thirlmere, formerly two lakes known as Leathes Water and Wythburn Water, and earlier still as Blackmere.

It was in 1875 that Manchester Corporation, with its growing demands for additional water, cast its covetous eyes on Thirlmere with the intention of turning a lake into a reservoir. Its level was raised by 50 feet by a great dam; its area was more than doubled; and from it the water now runs 95 miles into Manchester. Ruskin said that 'Manchester should be put to the bottom of Thirlmere, as it was trying to steal and sell the clouds of Helvellyn.'

WHITE SIDE

A substantial cairn marks the summit of White Side on the ascent from Thirlmere. From here we look across the Vale of Keswick to Skiddaw.

CALFHOW PIKE

Calfhow Pike forms part of the Helvellyn ridge and lies about a mile due south from Clough Head. In inclement weather a quick descent can be made from here via a steep path to Hill Top Farm in the Vale of St John.

CLOUGH HEAD SUMMIT

Clough Head is the name given to the most northerly summit of the ridge running south to Helvellyn. The path to it can be confusing in mist. Its summit is marked by a trig point and small shelter which can be used as a break against the wind. After descending Clough Head by White Pike and Mosedale Beck, we head northward to Wallthwaite.

CLOUGH HEAD FROM CASTLERIGG STONE CIRCLE

Cradled by the surrounding mountains, the great stone circle at Castlerigg, built around 3000 BC, is one of the most visually impressive and oldest prehistoric sites in the Lake District. It is also the most visited. Of the original forty-two stones that formed this megalithic stone circle, thirty-eight remain, forming the circle of about 100 feet in diameter. Archaeologists are of the opinion that the alignment of the stones may act as a stone calendar; sight-lines at sunrise would give various fixed dates in the year. Sometimes called the Carles, Castlerigg is the second largest stone circle in Cumbria, after Long Meg.

BLENCATHRA FROM TEWITT TARN

Blencathra, or Saddleback as it is more commonly referred to when viewed from the east, is one of the great mountains of the Lake District. Separated from Skiddaw by the wide valley of Glenderaterra Beck, it rises in a simple arc above Threlkeld. Its long top is a series of delicate peaks that descend from the summit in fine lateral spurs and swooping hollows. From the Moorland slopes of Naddle Fell, Tewitt Tarn makes a fitting foreground for Blencathra. The abundance of reeds provides nesting sites for a variety of waterfowl. Its name is derived from the Peewits that abound on the surrounding fells. The route to Blencathra via Scales Fell is the most common as well as being the easiest.

SHARP EDGE

Sharp Edge on Blencathra runs along the north side of Scales Tarn and is one of the narrowest ridges in the Lake District. Although not as long as Striding Edge on Helvellyn, it is steeper on both sides, falling 800 feet to the tarn below. In winter, when the mountain is covered in snow, it becomes a mountaineering challenge requiring careful negotiation and is not for the faint-hearted.

BLENCATHRA SUMMIT

Blencathra lies at the northern edge of the Lake District. From its summit cairn there are extensive views.

WHITE CROSS

On the plateau between the summit of Blencathra and Atkinson Pike there are two stone crosses to arouse the curiosity of fell walkers. The larger of these, made from white quartz-like rock set into the ground, is to the memory of Mr Staughan of Threlkeld, who was killed on active service in 1942. It was built by his friend Harold Robinson who, sometimes twice a day, climbed the fell from Threlkeld, each time carrying a stone for the cross. He died in 1988 at eighty years of age.

THRELKELD

Looking down the broad, smooth shoulder of Blease Fell to Threlkeld.

DAY THREE
WHIT MONDAY
25 May 1931

KESWICK TO BUTTERMERE

Forecast: *A cloudy morning followed by showers in the afternoon.*

From	To	Map ref.	Height	Mileage	Ascent	Descent
Keswick	Portinscale	NY 2505 2360	250	1	0	-270
Portinscale	Catbells	NY 2440 1990	1,400	2.5	1,150	0
Catbells	Maiden Moor	NY 2370 1820	1,888	1.25	700	-212
Maiden Moor	Eel Crags	NY 2345 1643	2,126	1.25	238	-115
Eel Crags	Dalehead Crags	NY 2260 1560	1,900	0.75	269	-380
Dalehead Crags	Dale Head	NY 2230 1530	2,473	0.75	573	0
Dale Head	Hindscarth	NY 2150 1575	2,385	1	265	-385
Hindscarth	Robinson	NY 2015 1685	2,419	1.5	559	-525
Robinson	Newlands Hause	NY 1930 1760	1,096	1	0	-1,323
Newlands Hause	Knott Rigg	NY 1965 1855	1,772	0.75	676	0
Knott Rigg	Ard Crags	NY 2060 1970	1,864	0.75	220	-128
Ard Crags	Sail	NY 1985 2035	2,400	1	874	-338
Sail	Crag Hill	NY 1931 2035	2,753	0.25	353	0
Crag Hill	Grasmoor	NY 1745 2030	2,791	1	161	-381
Grasmoor	Wandhope	NY 1880 1975	2,533	1	161	-419
Wandhope	Whiteless Pike	NY 1795 1895	2,159	0.75	256	-118
Whiteless Pike	Buttermere	NY 1750 1695	450	1.75	0	-1,709
	Totals for day			18.25	6,455	-6,303

KESWICK, 'METROPOLIS OF THE LAKES'

Situated on the River Greta at the northern extremity of the unseen Derwent Water, sheltered beneath the high slopes of Skiddaw, is this attractive old market town, where climbers, walkers and tourists rub shoulders in the confines of its narrow streets. In July they are joined by scores of clergymen and church people who converge on the town for the Keswick Convention. In the centre of the market place, on the site of an older building dating from Elizabethan times, stands the Moot Hall.

At the time of Elizabeth I the mining area around Keswick was the equivalent of the Canadian Klondike, and Keswick itself was the Dawson City of the age. The mining was placed in the expert hands of the Bavarians, who were considered the most advanced miners at that time.

In 1813 the old courthouse was pulled down and the German miners who worked here erected the present building, Tyrolean in mood, on the lines of a south German *stadthaus*. A diligent local winds the curiously single-handed clock in the tower every night.

CATBELLS FROM OVERSIDE WOOD

Catbells, that oddly named fell rising steeply from Derwent Water's western shore, belongs to the Newlands Valley and Mrs Tiggywinkle of Beatrix Potter fame, whose house was on the hillside above Little Town.

Its name is derived from 'cat bield', a place where wild cats shelter, and its popularity has become legendary. However, visitors should be aware that the open mine shafts which litter the fell on both flanks have given Catbells a reputation for minor accidents.

CATBELLS

The Catbells ridge has always been a popular walk with tourists from Keswick, many of whom do not venture much further. It justifies itself as a walk by having excellent views over Derwent Water, Borrowdale and Newlands Valley, which is exactly what the tourist requires.

THE JAWS OF BORROWDALE

At the southern end of Derwent Water, just beyond Grange, where the slopes of Grange Fell and Castle Crag come together to give scarcely enough room for the river and road to pass, lies the famous Jaws of Borrowdale. It was here, in one of the caves of Castle Crag, that Millican Dalton lived his strange lifestyle between the wars. Dressed in homemade clothes, he sailed the Derwent on a raft of his own construction, a 'hippy' before 'hippies' existed.

DERWENT WATER AND SKIDDAW FROM MAIDEN MOOR

Beyond the shapely ridge of Catbells, in the shadow of Skiddaw and Blencathra, the Vale of Keswick spreads outward to the sylvan beauty of Derwent Water, and its numerous islands. In the seventh century, St Herbert, a disciple of Cuthbert, the Northumbrian saint, came to live as a hermit on the largest of these islands, which later became known as St Herbert's Island. In the past it has enjoyed many romantic associations; Shelley, Coleridge, Southey and Ruskin all spent their honeymoons in the area.

MAIDEN MOOR PLATEAU

High country can rarely be appreciated properly from the bottom of valleys, and the long ridge above the small hamlet of Grange-in-Borrowdale is not a ridge, as it appears to be, but the edge of a wide, grassy plateau. Maiden Moor lies on the ridge that forms the western side of the Borrowdale Valley. The ascent is usually made from Hawse End as a ridge walk over Catbells.

CAUSEY PIKE

Causey Pike, whose knuckle-like ridge and prominent knob of a summit dominate the Newlands skyline, is one of Lakeland's most popular peaks. In 1864 E. L. Linton wrote, 'With its royal fatuous face, George the Third, double chin, snub nose, receding forehead and all, can be made out in the crowning knob of Causey Pike.' Like many of the fells around Newlands, it was once the scene of much mining activity.

EEL CRAGS

Eel Crags lies between Maiden Moor and Dalehead high above the Newlands Valley, the highest point of which is High Spy. From here we look across to Dale Head.

HIGH SPY SUMMIT

The summit of the ridge above Eel Crags is known as High Spy: a curious summit ringed by crags. Its western flank overlooks Borrowdale.

EEL CRAGS FROM DALE HEAD TARN

Causey Pike and the craggy profile of Eel Crags are seen here from Dale Head Tarn.

DALE HEAD CAIRN

In 1993, after years of vandalism, the summit cairn of Dale Head, perched on the very edge of its precipitous north face, was lovingly restored to its former glory by Ray McHaffie of Keswick.

DALE HEAD

Dale Head, guardian of the Vale of Newlands, is perhaps the easiest of all the high fells to ascend. Simply follow the old wire fence beginning opposite the youth hostel at Honister Hause. The summit, rounded and grassy, is topped with a beautiful cairn.

HONISTER PASS

The Honister Pass is the direct route between the head of Borrowdale and Buttermere. Starting at Seatoller in Borrowdale, the road rises, in parts at a gradient of one in four, to the summit at 1,176 feet. Immediately beyond the crest, the full downward sweep of Honister Crag bursts suddenly into view, presenting its almost perpendicular outline. Once notoriously dangerous, the descent, with its boulder-strewn verges meandering west alongside Gatesgarth Beck towards Buttermere, is now considered to be as safe as any road in the region.

ROBINSON SUMMIT

From the summit cairn of Robinson we look towards Crummock and Loweswater. The hamlet of Kirkstile nestles in the green fields lying between the two.

ROBINSON

At the western end of the ridge from Dale Head, Robinson, synonymous with Buttermere since the early nineteenth century when the proprietor of the Fish Inn shared the same name, is the least attractive of the Buttermere fells. Its name, however, comes from a former landowner. The broad, stony plateau of the summit gives extensive views: across Buttermere is the craggy face of the High Stile range; to the right is Mellbreak, beside Crummock Water; and Grasmoor appears north-west beyond Wandop, Sail and Grisedale Pike. The most interesting and scenic ascent is made from Newlands.

ARD CRAGS TO KNOTT RIGG

Looking southwest along the ridge to Knott Rigg from Ard Crags. High Stile and Red Pike dominate the skyline.

Above: **SAIL SUMMIT**
Sail is quite a good fell but better surround it. From its grassy summit, the ridge route to Crag Hill is easily defined.

Right: **CRAG HILL**
The trig point on Crag Hill. In early summer, Crag Hill has patches of alpine flowers growing on its rocky summit.

GRASMOOR SUMMIT

Grasmoor, with its eight tops, has the distinction of having the most extensive summit over 2,500 feet. As a mountain viewpoint it is without equal. To the south the Great Central Fells present an imposing front of receding ranges – High Stile, Pillar, Kirkfell, Great Gable, Great End, Scafell, Bowfell and Langdale.

WANDHOPE

Wandhope lies about a mile southwest of Crag Hill. From the ridge to Whiteless Pike we look back to the broad snow covered slopes of Wandhope and Thirdgill Head.

Right: **WHITELESS PIKE**

Whiteless Pike lies west of Wandhope, on the ridge that comes up from Buttermere. Its summit provides fine views over the Buttermere Valley to the High Stile ridge.

Below: As we descend from Whiteless Pike, Crummock and Loweswater come into view at Saddle Gate.

GRASMOOR FROM LANTHWAITE GREEN

The immense bulk of Grasmoor, always recognisable when seen from other fells, towers over the tiny hamlet of Lanthwaite Green where the early British had a large settlement. On 9 September 1760, a fearful storm arose over the Coledale Fells. An enormous torrent of water cascaded down the ravine of Gasgale Gill, between Whiteside and Brackenthwaite Fell, and burst over Lanthwaite Green with devastating results, laying waste to 10 acres with mud and stone wrenched from the sides of the mountains.

CRUMMOCK WATER AND RANNERDALE KNOTTS

The black shoulder of Rannerdale Knotts, with its mile-long knuckle-like ridge, seems to hang over the east shore of Crummock Water. Legend has it that Rannerdale, the little dale running alongside the Knotts, was the only part of England not conquered by the invading Normans. Often referred to as the Secret Valley, it is well known for bluebells, which carpet the dale in the spring. Crummock Water takes its name from the Norse word for crumpled or bent, appertaining to cows having that kind of horn. The late Canon Rawnsley mentions the Norse chieftain Buthar as having given the district its name of Butter-mere, and Sour Milk Ghyll would seem to bear this out. The fells that surround Crummock are graceful and much less rugged than other areas of the Lake District, and the indented shore competes with Buttermere for beauty.

Above: **ST JAMES' CHURCH, BUTTERMERE**

Set on a rocky outcrop surrounded by the magnificent Buttermere scenery is the tiny Church of St James. It was built in 1846 to replace the nearby chapel of Brigham. Across the valley, the waterfall of Sour Milk Ghyll cascades down from Bleaberry Tarn into the calm waters of Buttermere.

Inset: **WAINWRIGHT MEMORIAL**

Set into the alcove of the south window is a memorial tablet dedicated to the legendary fell walker Alfred Wainwright, whose pictorial guidebooks with their hand-drawn maps sold in their millions. The window looks out onto Haystacks, where, at his request, his ashes were scattered at the edge of Innominate Tarn.

BUTTERMERE

Ringed on three sides by mountains, including the dramatic peaks of Grasmoor, Haystacks, Fleetwith Pike and Mellbreak, the Buttermere Valley at the western end of the Honister Pass is the only Lakeland valley to possess three lakes: Buttermere, Crummock and Loweswater.

Reminiscent of a Norwegian fjord, Buttermere is separated from Crummock by a strip of low-lying land half a mile wide. In the distant past they were undoubtedly one lake.

DAY FOUR
TUESDAY
26 May 1931

BUTTERMERE TO WASDALE

Forecast: *Bright all day.*

From	To	Map ref.	Height	Mileage	Ascent	Descent
Buttermere	Red Pike (via Ruddy Beck)	NY 1605 1545	2,479	2	2,029	0
Red Pike	High Stile	NY 1675 1475	2,644	0.75	301	-136
High Stile	High Crag	NY 1805 1415	2,395	1	0	-249
High Crag	Scarth Gap	NY 1893 1330	1,450	0.75	0	-945
Scarth Gap	Haystacks	NY 1935 1315	1,946	0.5	496	0
Haystacks	Blackbeck Tarn	NY 2090 1215	1,598	0.5	0	-348
Blackbeck Tarn	Brandreth	NY 2150 1195	2,344	1.25	496	0
Brandreth	Green Gable	NY 2150 1075	2,527	0.75	391	-208
Green Gable	Windy Gap	NY 2145 1055	2,400	0.25	0	-127
Windy Gap	Great Gable	NY 2115 1035	2,949	0.25	549	0
Great Gable	Kirk Fell	NY 1990 1075	2,630	1	593	-912
Kirk Fell	Black Sail Pass	NY1915 1145	1,798	0.5	0	-832
Black Sail Pass	Looking Stead	NY 1860 1180	2,058	0.5	260	0
Looking Stead	Pillar	NY 1715 1210	2,927	1	869	0
Pillar	(detour via Pillar Rock)	NY 1725 1235	2,905	0.5	0	-22
Pillar Rock	Wind Gap	NY 1685 1175	2,450	0.25	22	-477
Wind Gap	Scoat Fell	NY 1600 1135	2,749	1	299	0
Scoat Fell	Red Pike	NY 1655 1055	2,730	1	180	-199
Red Pike	Dore Head	NY 1747 9450	1,250	0.75	0	-1,480
Dore Head	Wasdale Head	NY 1863 0875	256	1.5	0	-994
	Totals for day			16	6,485	-6,929

GRASMOOR AND CRUMMOCK
Red Pike in Buttermere lies at the western end of the High Stile ridge that divides Buttermere from Ennerdale. The view from the summit is almost equal to that of Grasmoor, seen here across Crummock Water. One particular feature is the number of lakes, which appear in every direction across the wide vista.

RED PIKE SUMMIT
The High Stile range begins in the west with Great Borne and continues along the ridge to Starling Dodd and Red Pike. One of the rarely stressed attributes of this ridge is its suitability for an introduction to ridge walking. As we pause on the summit we look north across Dodd to Newlands Hause, Robinson and Blencathra.

HIGH STILE

From High Stile we look down on Bleaberry Tarn, The Saddle and Mellbreak. On the right the north-western fell of Grasmoor towers high above Crummock Water.

NORTHERN FELLS FROM HIGH STILE

Separated by a narrow ridge, the parallel valleys of Ennerdale and Buttermere are worlds apart in appearance. Ennerdale, where the Liza flows through large conifer plantations, is a barren valley, while the Vale of Buttermere has two lakes, Buttermere and Crummock. The central and highest point of the ridge, which includes Red Pike and High Crag, is High Stile at 2644 feet. Scarped by the precipitous crags of Bleaberry and Birkness Combs, the extensive panorama from the summit culminates on the distant Blencathra.

BURTNESS COMB
Burtness Comb is well known by rock climbers for its variety of crags. From its summit we look north to Blencathra, Robinson, Dale Head and Fleetwith Pike.

SCARTH GAP
On descending High Crag we cross Scarth Gap, which is the principle pass from Buttermere to Ennerdale, the jagged outline of Haystacks before us.

HAYSTACKS

Haystacks is a continuation of Fleetwith Pike, curving round to enclose Warnscale Bottom at the head of Buttermere. Its serrated top, one of the roughest in the district, is not a good place to be in mist, and should be avoided in bad weather because of its precipitous sides.

This was Wainwright's favourite mountain where his ashes were scattered by his widow Betty. In his memoir *Ex-Fellwanderer* he writes, 'And if you, dear reader, should get a bit of grit in your boots as you are crossing Haystacks in the years to come, please treat it with respect. It might be me.'

INNOMINATE TARN

In a quiet and lonely place, set amongst the hummocks and craggy outcrops of the Haystacks plateau, lies the unnamed tarn – the Innominate. In its wild setting, it poses a fine foreground for Pillar and Great Gable across the valley. This was Wainwright's favourite peak where his ashes were scattered by his wife Betty.

There is a hill that stands for me / Beyond the sunset and the sea, / A ladder of light ascending; / when I have crossed the evening ray / and lost my comrade of white day. / It beckons to me, bending / a mountain-way of wind and rain / to draw my feet from the dark plain:- / Where stars of slumber kindle on its crest, / my hill, the high hill, from wandering to rest.

Geoffrey Winthrop-Young

BLACKBECK TARN

Cradled in a hollow and surrounded on all sides by rocky outcrops, Blackbeck Tarn is the largest of the tarns on Haystacks. It measures about 750 feet from north to south, and 300 feet east to west. The outlet stream from the tarn plunges in a series of cascades to Warnscale Bottom, 1,000 feet below.

ENNERDALE AND BUTTERMERE FROM MOSES TROD

All climbers and walkers who have visited Gable Crag from Wasdale or Buttermere have entered into the environment of Moses.

A well-defined track of uncertain antiquity runs up Gavel Neese from Wasdale, turns left at the prominent boulder known as 'Moses' Finger', crosses Beckhead and the face of Gable Crag, rounds the shoulders of Green Gable and Brandreth, until, finally, it reaches the Honister Pass. The path, an old smugglers' route, is known as 'Moses Trod'. From our vantage point near Brandreth we look down on the Buttermere and Ennerdale valleys.

PILLAR AND ENNERDALE

Looking west from Moses Trod we have one of the most commanding views of Pillar and Ennerdale. Beyond the Black Sail Pass, and beneath Looking Stead, the handiwork of the Forestry Commission becomes evident; dark conifers carpet the valley floor for almost 6 miles, while below our feet the river Liza snakes through the thick plantations and into Ennerdale Water.

GREEN GABLE – GREAT GABLE

Green Gable, divided from Great Gable by Windy Gap, is probably visited only as a means of reaching its mightier neighbour. That said, the broad, rounded peak offers tremendous views of the surrounding fells and the precipitous northern face of Great Gable. For the walker who is not ashamed to motor to the top of Honister, it is an easy ascent.

WINDY GAP

It has been suggested that in Neolithic times, Windy Gap, the short shaley col between Green Gable and Great Gable, may have been used as a pack route ferrying stone axes from the factories in Langdale, to the coastal settlements where they were exported.

TOPHET BASTION

Looking up the scree run of Great Hell Gate the solitary rock fang of Hell Gate Pillar acts as sentinel to the rock wall of Tophet Bastion.

NAPES NEEDLE

Some of the most popular rock climbing in the district can be found on the ridges known as Napes below the summit of Great Gable. Situated at the western end of the Gable Traverse near Great Hell Gate is the dramatic pinnacle of Napes Needle. This isolated crag has done more than anything else to popularise British rock climbing. It was first climbed alone in June 1886 by W. P. Haskett-Smith, who repeated his climb in Easter 1936 at the age of seventy-six to celebrate the Jubilee.

SPHINX ROCK

Continuing along the traverse we reach the aptly named Sphinx Rock, which gazes inscrutably over the mosaic patchwork of fields in Wasdale Head far below.

Right: **WESTMORLAND CAIRN**

Perched on a rock platform south of Great Gable summit is the Westmorland Cairn. It was built in 1876 by the Westmorland brothers to indicate what they regarded as Lakeland's finest view, showing Wastwater to the southwest and the Scafell Pike range across the great gulf of Upper Wasdale to the southeast. From our viewpoint below Westmorland Crags we look eastwards to Sprinkling Tarn and the Langdale Pikes.

Below: **WASDALE FROM GREAT GABLE**

Great Gable has one distinct advantage over most of the Lakeland fells: it can be climbed direct from each of the five surrounding valleys, namely Wasdale, Eskdale, Langdale, Borrowdale and Buttermere. From the summit slopes we look down on a jumble of small fields half a mile below.

FELL AND ROCK MEMORIAL

A short walk over the boulder-strewn plateau of Great Gable leads to the summit where the war memorial plaque of the Fell and Rock Climbing Club is set into the rocks facing north. This plaque of bronze, engraved with a relief map of the neighbouring peaks and the names of the twenty members killed in the Great War, was purchased by the club and presented to the nation through the National Trust. The peaks indicated are Allen Crags, Base Brown, Brandreth, Broad Crag, Green Gable, Great Gable, Great End, Grey Knott, Glaramara, Kirkfell, Lingmell and Seathwaite Fell.

On 8 June 1924, these summit rocks were draped with a war-stained Union Jack that had flown from HMS *Barnham* at the Battle of Jutland. In the grey mist and softly falling rain, some 500 climbers, walkers and dales-folk assembled here to witness the unveiling of the bronze tablet. Each year on Remembrance Sunday hundreds of walkers gather for a silent ceremony on the summit.

BECK HEAD TARNS AND KIRKFELL FROM GREAT GABLE

Kirkfell, isolated between Great Gable and Pillar, offers no easy ascent, and the track, which follows the remains of a fence line from Beck Head to the summit plateau, is a rough and tedious course.

Overshadowed by the vast scree falls of Great Gable, the two tarns of Beck Head are on the col below. Fed by underground springs, they are within a few feet of each other, however, the smaller of the two is seasonal and cannot really by termed a true tarn.

BLACK SAIL PASS, SUMMIT COL

The Black Sail Pass, linking Wasdale to Ennerdale, skirts the flanks of Kirkfell and winds gradually up to the col at 2,443 feet, before descending into Ennerdale towards Cumbria's remotest youth hostel, the Black Sail Hut.

ENNERDALE, FROM LOOKING STEAD

The High Stile ridge begins in the west at Great Bourne, rising to the higher Red Pike, High Stile and High Crag, before descending to the col at Scarth Gap. From our viewpoint at Looking Stead we look across Ennerdale to the barren slopes of this long ridge.

ROBINSON CAIRN

The cairn, which stands at the end of the high-level route to the summit of Pillar, was built by members of the Fell and Rock Climbing Club on Saturday, 13 June 1908. This was as a memorial to John Wilson Robinson, a pioneer rock climber who, on 27 June 1882, in heavy mist and rain, made his first ascent of Pillar Rock. As a mountaineer he was magnificent at route finding; he had that rare gift of being able to read a mountain like a book. On a rock face near to the cairn is a bronze memorial tablet dedicated to him.

PILLAR ROCK

This isolated crag on the precipitous breast of Pillar mountain was once regarded as being unclimbable. The remoteness and inaccessibility of its summit has for over 100 years held a fascination for both walker and climber. Early guidebooks clothed it with a certain amount of mystery and awe. The first known ascent was made in 1826 by John Atkinson, a shepherd from Croftfoot in Ennerdale, up the route now known as the 'Old West Climb', and by 1870 the first lady had scaled the 'unclimbable' Pillar.

The discovery of the 65-foot Pendlebury Traverse on the east face of High Man was made by Richard Pendlebury, who, after walking from Keswick in his smoke room slippers, climbed directly up from the Slab; a painful experience which has yet to be repeated. The best and shortest approach is from Wasdale Head via the high-level route.

ENNERDALE WATER AND PILLAR

Ennerdale, the most westerly of all, is the longest and most desolate of the mountain valleys, and the only one not accessible by road. It is surrounded by the precipitous slopes of Kirkfell, Pillar, and Steeple on one side, and High Crag, High Stile and Red Pike on the other. At its head, rising above the dark conifer plantations, is the magnificent dome of Great Gable. From our viewpoint by the lake we can see the distinctive lines of Pillar Rock and Steeple.

DORE HEAD AND STIRRUP CRAG

On descending Red Pike in the direction of Wasdale, we come to Dore Head and Stirrup Crag, an awkward scramble up the northern extremity of Yewbarrow. Here the gentle slopes of Gosforth Crag and Over Beck contrast sharply with the spectacular views into Mosedale and Wasdale Head.

61

DAY FIVE
WEDNESDAY
27 May 1931

WASDALE TO LANGDALE

Forecast: *Bright in the morning and afternoon turning to thunder and overcast in the evening.*

From	To	Map ref.	Height	Mileage	Ascent	Descent
Wasdale Head	Brown Tongue	NY 1990 0735	750	1.25	494	0
Brown Tongue	Scafell Pike	NY 2155 0725	3,206	1.5	2,456	0
Scafell Pike	(detour via Mickledore Chasm)	NY 2095 0690	2,566	0.5	0	-640
Mickledore Chasm	Broad Crag	NY 2185 0754	2,948	0.75	554	-156
Broad Crag	Great End	NY 2267 0838	2,984	1	176	-140
Great End	Esk Hause	NY 2330 0805	2,477	0.5	0	-507
Esk Hause	Esk Pike	NY 2367 0752	2,830	0.5	353	0
Esk Pike	Ore Gap	NY 2405 0720	2,600	0.25	0	-230
Ore Gap	Bowfell	NY 2447 0644	2,750	0.5	150	0
Bowfell	Three Tarns	NY 2480 0605	2,360	0.5	0	-390
Three Tarns	Shelter Crags	NY 2497 0533	2,637	0.25	277	0
Shelter Crags	Crinkle Crags	NY 2486 0486	2,733	0.25	96	0
Crinkle Crags	Cold Pike	NY 2628 0361	2,259	1.5	120	-594
Cold Pike	Red Tarn	NY 2680 0370	1,726	1	0	-533
Red Tarn	Pike O' Blisco	NY 2711 0421	2,286	0.5	560	0
Pike O' Blisco	Blake Rigg	NY 2852 0390	1,760	1.25	0	-526
Blake Rigg	Wall End	NY 2835 0550	354	1	0	-1,406
Wall End	Old Dungeon Ghyll Hotel	NY 2860 0615	325	0.5	0	-29
	Totals for day			13.5	5,236	-5,151

Above: **GREAT GABLE FROM DOWN IN THE DALE**

Great Gable, symbol of the National Park, Mecca of Lakeland walkers. Although Scafell Pike is the highest in England, it is generally accepted that there is no mountain in the Lake District worth climbing more than Great Gable, whose summit commands widespread panoramas. When viewed from down the dale it appears as a giant pyramid at the head of the lake, standing separate from the mountains on either side, but to see the fell at its best you must climb to the summit of Lingmell.

Right: **THE SCREES**

It is difficult to describe one's reaction on first seeing the Screes. They spread like a great fan, sheer from their precipitous cliffs, downward into the waters in which their reflection often carries for a further 258 feet.

It is told that in the nineteenth century a buttress known as Wilson's Horse, 'a girt lump as big as Manchester town hall', came crashing down into the lake with a mighty roar, and a great 'tidal wave' swept up the valley. The noise was so terrible at Wasdale Head that the end of the world was deemed to be nigh, and a special service was held in the church. Yet even this made little change to the contours of the screes.

WASDALE FROM LINGMELL GILL

Almost entirely enclosed by the highest peaks in England, Wasdale, wild and austere, is the most inaccessible dale in the Lake District. The valley floor, intersected by stone walls, is a mosaic of grassy enclosures. From the lower slopes of Lingmell we look across the valley to Mosedale, the hamlet of Wasdale Head and the crags of Pillar.

BROWN TONGUE AND SCAFELL

Standing at the foot of Brown Tongue, between the two branches of Lingmell Beck, you will find yourself staring upwards to the great craggy bastion of Scafell, towering above. At the top of the Tongue you will come to the boulder-strewn cove of Hollow Stones, between Lingmell and Black Crag, leading to the ridge of Mickledore.

MICKLEDORE AND SCAFELL CRAGS FROM LINGMELL

Lingmell is a mountain on which to linger until evening, for it is then, with the sun illuminating its precipitous northern face, that Scafell becomes most striking. The crag on the left is Pulpit Rock, and across the connecting arête of Mickledore is the vertical fang of Pisgah. Next is the Pinnacle and Deep Ghyll Buttress, and finally Scafell Summit.

GREAT GABLE FROM LINGMELL ARÊTE

Lingmell Crag lies less than a mile from Scafell. Its situation is dramatic and its views extensive. On reaching the summit, marked by a very tall and slender cairn at the edge of the arête, one's eye is immediately drawn to the tremendous southern façade of Great Gable, rising with an illusion of sheerness that seems impossible to climb.

PIERS GHYLL

Piers Ghyll owes its notoriety to an accident that occurred in the summer of 1921, when Mr Crump, a visitor from London, lost his way while walking in mist from Coniston to Wasdale Head. On 21 June he was unlucky enough to get into Piers Ghyll and sustain an injury to his leg. He was to remain there without food for the following twenty days until he was rescued by a party of rock climbers attempting a descent of the Ghyll. After descending several small pitches, they found Mr Crump just below Bridge Rock, sitting sideways and gazing down the Ghyll. After a difficult descent using ropes and a stretcher, Mr Crump was successfully conveyed to the Wasdale Hotel.

MICKLEDORE AND HOLLOW STONES

Beneath Pikes Crag lies the area known as Hollow Stones. This and the Mickledore ridge are overlooked by the dark buttress of Scafell Crag. This is a foolhardy route if the weather is not perfect.

PIKES CRAG FROM MICKLEDORE

To the left of Mickledore, forming a shoulder of Scafell Pike, is Pikes Crag and Pulpit Rock; unfortunately this fine crag suffers from its proximity to Scafell.

SCAFELL CRAG FROM BROAD CRAG TARN

According to W. Heaton-Cooper, the word 'tarn' is derived from the old Norse word 'tjorn', meaning a small lake or teardrop. There are in total almost 500 of these 'teardrops' scattered across the fells, and while a few are only a short distance from the roads, most lie hidden in the folds of the fells above the intake walls, nestling like jewels in the heart of an ancient castle.

Noted for being the highest tarn in Lakeland, Broad Crag Tarn lies 2,746 feet above sea level, half a mile from the summit of Scafell Pike. The broad flat shelf on which it is situated contrasts sharply with the profile of Scafell's Central Buttress where some of the most difficult climbs are to be found.

BROAD STAND

The first recorded descent from the summit of Scafell by way of Broad Stand was made accidentally in August 1802 by Samuel Taylor Coleridge, who at the time suffered a terrible palsy of the limbs. It has since been argued that it was not Broad Stand that Coleridge negotiated, but the nearby Mickledore Chimney, which is even more difficult.

The route now may be well worn, but unless you are experienced it is wise to turn back; remember that under icy conditions the lower part of Broad Stand is an impossible route for the fell walker.

FOXES TARN

In a hanging valley, just below the summit of Scafell, lies Foxes Tarn. This tiny pool, the smallest to be given a name, is the second-highest tarn in Lakeland. From here we look across to the summit of Scafell Pike.

SCAFELL PIKE, SUMMIT SHELTER

A stony track across a wilderness of grey rocks leads to the huge crumbling cairn of Scafell Pike, England's highest peak. A tablet of Honister slate, built facing north into the cairn, records that the summit was given to the nation by Baron Leconfield in 1919 as a memorial to the men of Lakeland who fell in the Great War of 1914–18.

SCAFELL PIKE, SUMMIT VIEW

In August 1922, His Royal Highness the Prince Consort of the Netherlands, in the company of George Abraham, became the first member of a royal family to ascend Scafell Pike, the highest point in England.

The view from the summit is one of mountains rather than lakes, with the shapely shoulder of Great Gable reaching down to Sty Head Tarn and Seathwaite Fell, then Green Gable, Base Brown and Glaramara, finally, to complete the picture, Derwent Water, Skiddaw and Blencathra.

LAMBFOOT DUB

The little tarn of Lambfoot Dub is situated on a broad shelf below the prominent peak of Long Pike and can be reached from the ridge path between Broad Crag and Scafell Pike. The tarn, or dub, filled with sparkling clear water, owes its name to its irregular shape: that of a lamb's foot. Across the valley to the northwest, Great Gable rises majestically against the skyline.

GREAT END AND THE CORRIDOR ROUTE

The Corridor Route from Sty Head is the easiest way of approaching Scafell Pike. From Great Gable it can be seen ascending obliquely across the lower slopes of Great End and the northerly buttress of the Scafell massif, before crossing Skew Gill and Piers Ghyll on its way to the summit.

GREAT END, CENTRAL GULLY

The view from the south exit of Central Gully, a 1,000 feet above the dark waters of Sprinkling Tarn, is one of the finest in Lakeland. The small sheet of water on Seathwaite Fell is High House Tarn. Grains Gill is on the right of the fell, winding its way through Borrowdale.

GREAT END, CENTRAL GULLY IN WINTER

When approached from Grains Gill, Great End is an awesome sight; with its broken buttresses and deep-cut gullies it towers above Sprinkling Tarn. When winter comes the snow lies deeper and longer than anywhere else, and the huge rift known as Central Gully, probably the most famous snow and ice climb in the Lake District, glistens white against a black buttress.

ESK HAUSE

It is an easy walk from Great End to Esk Hause; well defined, it is one of the main arteries of the western fells. It is only in winter, when a mantle of snow covers the ground, that Esk Hause bursts into activity; here the snow lies deeper and longer than anywhere else.

ESK HAUSE CROSSROADS

The famous crossroads at Esk Hause, frequented by thousands of fell walkers, is the Piccadilly Circus of Lakeland. For the strong walker it can be used a starting point; however, walks from here should not be undertaken lightly, especially in less-than-perfect weather, and ramblers should keep their compasses in hand. From the shelter, Esk Pike rises almost due south and the route is unmistakable, but the long high ridge of Bowfell cannot be seen until you ascend the rough slopes of Ewer Gap.

ORE GAP

North-west of Bowfell the main ridge drops to the depression of Ore gap, a narrow col between Esk Pike and Bowfell, where the ground is stained red due to the presence of hematite. On the north side, below the col and in a secluded hollow, is Angle Tarn. Beyond the Gap the ridge makes a stony ascent to the summit of Esk Pike.

BOWFELL SUMMIT CAIRN

Bowfell's summit is a mass of rocks and shattered boulders, a place for twisting ankles. Its main cairn and that of the southern summit are very small affairs, particularly when taking into account the readily available supply of building material.

BOWFELL SUMMIT VIEW

Lying at the head of Langdale, Bowfell is one of the truly great mountains of the Lake District. From its summit we look across to Pike O' Blisco and the Langdale Valley.

CRINKLE CRAGS

Descending Bowfell we come to one of the finest mountain ridges in Britain. Crinkle Crags is a switchback over the rocky lumps that give the fell its name. The going is rough underfoot but there is only the well-known 'Bad Step' to negotiate before descending to Red Tarn.

ROSSETT GILL

Eroded by the boots of generations, Rossett Gill, one of the longest and most arduous ascents in the Lake District, climbs for almost 2,000 feet in less than a mile to link Langdale and Scafell with the Wasdale fells. James Payn, when writing of his visits to the Lake District in 1865, caustically observed that the ascent 'must be made on all fours'. The knee-jarring descent into Langdale is a route for masochists only.

BOWFELL FROM LONG TOP

The highest summit of the Crinkles is Long Top at 2,826 feet. On attaining it, the eye is led northwards over Shelter Crags to this classic view of Bowfell, about a mile distant. Its southern face, broken by a daunting series of gullies, is known as the Bowfell links.

Left: **THE BAD STEP**
Caution is needed on the descent southward from the summit. It is a steep path down a slope of loose scree to a chock-stone blocking the gully. The impasse is avoided and the gully regained by an awkward descent of rock wall, which deserves the name 'the Bad Step'.

Below: **COLD PIKE SUMMIT**
Cold Pike lies between the Three Shires Stone on the Wrynose Pass and Crinkle Crags. The summit is three rocky humps, each with a cairn and sprinkled with boulders. From the main summit there is a magnificent view over Little Langdale to Windermere and the distant Pennines.

BLAKE RIGG SUMMIT

At the eastern extremity of Pike O' Blisco, just below the rocky summit of Blake Rigg, a broad shelf provides a convenient platform for a magnificent vista over Little Langdale Tarn to Windermere.

LANGDALES FROM BLAKE RIGG

If you climb the slopes of Blake Rigg above Blea Tarn, you are rewarded with a beautiful view of the Langdale Pikes.

BLEA TARN AND LINGMOOR

On the descent from Blake Rigg summit, Blea Tarn comes into view. In the foreground is Lingmoor, with the Helvellyn range on the horizon.

RED TARN

Above the Wrynose summit, on the gentle grassy slopes of the col dividing Cold Pike from Pike O' Blisco, Red Tarn, with its fringe of reeds, sits in splendid isolation. For its size it is extremely shallow, and its gentle contours contrast with the rugged crags of Great Knott, Crinkle Crags and Bowfell. In the nineteenth century, a whisky smuggler named Lanty Slee was supposed to have had an illicit still in the area.

Right: **BLEA TARN**

Described by Wordsworth as 'a liquid pool that glittered in the sun', this lovely tarn, fringed by juniper and rhododendron, lies in a hollow beneath Blake Rigg on the connecting road between Great and Little Langdale. It is a perfect setting from which to view the Langdale Pikes.

Below: **THE CRINKLES AND BOWFELL FROM PIKE O' BLISCO**

The serrated crest of Crinkle Crags is a conspicuous feature of the Langdale skyline. The Crinkles, of which there are five, are masses of rough rock and precipitous buttresses seamed with gullies. They provide a popular and spectacular way to Bowfell, on the same ridge. From Pike O' Blisco we look across Oxendale to the Crinkles and Bowfell.

LANGDALE PIKES FROM LINGMOOR TARN

On the eastern slopes of Lingmoor is a gem of a tarn. Lying in a hollow of bracken and heather, overgrown with reeds, Lingmoor Tarn and its large island are easily reached from either of the two Dungeon Ghyll Hotels. Lingmoor plays an important part in Wordsworth's *Excursion*, for the abode of the Solitary lies at the base of the fell.

SIDE PIKE AND THE LANGDALES

For visitors making their first visit to Langdale, there is no better place to view the region than from the shapely summit of Side Pike at the western extremity of Lingmoor, on the ridge connecting with Pike O' Blisco. The direct ascent is by way of Bleatarn House, but an easier route is from the gate just beyond Wall End.

Above: **LANGDALE MASSIF**

In the Lake District there are some forty mountains which are higher than the Langdale Pikes, but few leave such an indelible impression upon the mind. From Pike O' Blisco the entire east face of this mountain group is revealed in its true perspective. The thimble-shaped summit to the left is Pike O' Stickle, to the far right is Harrison Stickle, and between the two is the precipitous buttress of Gimmer Crag.

Right: **OLD DUNGEON GHYLL HOTEL**

Situated at the head of the Langdale Valley, the O.D.G. was formerly a farm and old coaching inn. In the latter part of the nineteenth century, it became a Mecca for climbers such as W. Haskett-Smith and the Abraham brothers.

DAY SIX
THURSDAY
28 May 1931

LANGDALE TO WINDERMERE

Forecast: *Cloudy and overcast all day.*
Rain by evening.

From	To	Map ref.	Height	Mileage	Ascent	Descent
Old Dungeon Ghyll Hotel	New Dungeon Ghyll Hotel	NY 2920 0650	315	0.5	0	-10
New Dungeon Ghyll Hotel	Dungeon Ghyll Force	NY 2900 0655	1,200	0.5	885	0
Dungeon Ghyll Force	Pike O' Stickle	NY 2739 0735	2,286	1	1,086	0
Pike O' Stickle	Harrison Stickle	NY 2818 0739	2,403	0.5	353	-236
Harrison Stickle	Pavey Ark	NY 2845 0790	2,288	0.5	0	-115
Pavey Ark	Sergeant Man	NY 2864 0889	2,300	1.5	12	0
Sergeant Man	High Raise	NY 2807 0953	2,500	0.5	200	0
High Raise	Greenup Edge	NY 2860 1055	1,581	0.75	0	-919
Greenup Edge	Calf Crag	NY 3016 1041	1,699	1	149	-30
Calf Crag	Gibson Knott	NY 3220 0990	1,290	1.25	0	-409
Gibson Knott	Helm Crag	NY 3266 0930	1,306	0.75	16	0
Helm Crag	Grasmere	NY 3770 0765	223	2	0	-1,083
Grasmere	Red Bank	NY 3390 0585	571	1.5	348	0
Red Bank	Loughrigg Terrace	NY 3405 0565	480	0.25	0	-91
Loughrigg Terrace	Pelter Bridge	NY 3635 0615	170	2	0	310
Pelter Bridge	Ambleside	NY 3770 0450	157	1	0	-27
	Totals for day			15.5	3,049	-2,610

Bus to Windermere

**_Above:_ NEW DUNGEON GHYLL
HOTEL**
The New Dungeon Ghyll Hotel and the
Sticklebarn Tavern have become popular
meeting places for climbers and ramblers
needing refreshment.

Right: DUNGEON GHYLL FORCE
A few minutes' walk from the New Hotel, in
a deep rift between Thorn Crag and Harrison
Stickle, is the waterfall from which it takes its
name. Dungeon Ghyll, hidden from general
view, should not be confused with the stream
that issues from Stickle Tarn and plunges down
the fellside in a series of cataracts to Langdale
Beck. This is Mill Ghyll (Stickle Gill), passed
on the ascent to Pavey Ark. According to
Wordsworth, Dungeon Ghyll Force 'is most
beautiful when it forms a silver thread'.

LANGDALE FROM PIKE HOW

The russet tints of autumn bracken contrast sharply with the verdant valley floor of Great Langdale, through which the beck meanders to Elterwater in the distance. The Low Wood Hotel can be seen on the edge of Lake Windermere.

HARRISON STICKLE FROM PIKE HOW

From Harrison Stickle, a long, grassy slope leads down past the ravine of Dungeon Ghyll to Pike How. In late October, before the onset of winter, the sheep are brought down from the high fell to lower pastures, surprising fell walkers on their way.

LOFT CRAG

Loft Crag, standing between Thorn Crag and Pike O' Stickle, is a prominent feature in the outline of the Langdale Pikes. Nearly all the views from the Windermere side give the impression that the Crag is part of Pike O' Stickle, but it is actually a separate peak jutting out from Harrison Stickle. The south-east face, known as Gimmer Crag, is popular with climbers as it provides the maximum exposure with the minimum risk.

HERDWICK SHEEP

Native only to the Lake District, the Herdwick is an exceptionally hardy breed that is able to survive on the high fells all year round. In monastic times, the herd-wyck was the sheep farm itself, not the sheep. The origin of this unique breed is not known, but it is thought that the Norsemen brought this sheep with them.

According to Canon Rawnsley, the medieval way of counting sheep was still in use in 1911, and the North American Indians apparently used similar numbers: 1, yan; 2, tyan; 3, tethera; 4, methera; 5, pimp; 6, sethera; 7, lethera; 8, hovera; 9, dorva; 10, dick; 11, yan-a-dick; 12, tyan-a-dick; 13, tethera-a-dick; 14, methera-a-dick; 15, bumfit; 16, yan-a-bumfit; 17, tyan-a-bumfit; 18, tethera-a-bumfit; 19, methera-a-bumfit; 20, giggot.

Left: PIKE O' STICKLE

Half a mile west of Harrison Stickle, the striated, beehive-shaped summit of Pike O' Stickle tops the steepest part of the Langdale face. In the rock face of the eastern Stone Shoot is a cave known as the Stone Axe Factory, where the Neolithic people made and polished axes that were widely exported. In exchange they received yew, coppiced from mainland Europe and used in the making of longbows. Centuries later, an order by Henry VIII made it compulsory for the statesmen of the Lake District to plant a yew tree by their homestead so that there would not be a lack of wood for making bows.

Below: PIKE O' STICKLE, SUMMIT VIEW

The summit of Pike O' Stickle yields an extensive panorama. Here we look towards Pinnacle Bield, Glaramara and Skiddaw.

Above: **HARRISON STICKLE FROM PIKE O' STICKLE**

Harrison Stickle is the higher of the two summits, being some 80 feet higher than Pike O' Stickle and separated from it by a distance of half a mile. The most popular and easiest ascent is via the path on the west side of Dungeon Ghyll, which approaches the summit from the north-west.

Right: **PAVEY ARK FROM HARRISON STICKLE**

Viewed from Harrison Stickle, Pavey Ark is seen in profile with its cliffs plunging down in a series of buttresses and gullies to Stickle Tarn.

PAVEY ARK

The enormous bow-shaped crag of Pavey Ark with its fearsome precipices forms the south-facing part of the Langdale Pikes. The most convenient approach is to follow the tourist path up the left side of Mill Gill, the overflow from Stickle Tarn, which falls into Great Langdale. Running obliquely from right to left across the face is the notorious ascent known as Jack's Rake; its line is easily traced above the dark waters of Stickle Tarn.

A covering of snow makes a postcard scene of Pavey Ark and Harrison Stickle.

SERGEANT MAN SUMMIT

North of the Langdale Pikes, a long, undulating ridge over high fells takes us in the direction of Keswick. Between Pavey Ark and Greenup Edge a small series of spurs and valleys lead on towards Grasmere. From the summit we look towards the Scafells and Great Gable.

THE LANGDALE VALLEY

Like Borrowdale, Langdale rivals in the popularity stakes with visitors to the Lake District. It is primarily a walkers' and climbers' valley. A narrow road, sandwiched between drystone walls, winds its way through the valley to Little Langdale. To the west and north an effectual barrier is created by the serrated edge of Crinkle Crags; the Crags, Bowfell, and the Langdale Pikes all display their full stature to the greatest advantage. Youdell Tarn, lying on the western side of the ridge separating Great Langdale from Easedale below Castle How, was reputed to contain trout in years gone by, but with the continual encroachment of reeds this now seems unlikely.

Left: HIGH RAISE SUMMIT LOOKING TOWARDS BOWFELL

High Raise is the moorland plateau that stretches north from the Langdale Pikes to Greenup Edge. On some maps it is described as High White Stones, which is a little to the north. High Raise is generally considered to be the centre of the Lake District.

Below: GREENUP EDGE LOOKING TO HELVELLYN AND FAIRFIELD

Greenup Edge is the depression between Ullscarf and High Raise. From the summit the view looks over the upper part of the Wythburn Valley down to Helm Crag and Grasmere.

Above: **CALF CRAG SUMMIT**
The northern rim of Far Easedale is a
short ridge walk running down from
Calf Crag over Gibson Knott to Helm
Crag. Three summits are traversed over
a distance of 2 miles. The summit of
Calf Crag looks down on the desolate
Wythburn Valley, probably the boggiest
valley in the Lake District.

Right: **GIBSON KNOTT
SUMMIT**
From the summit of Gibson Knott we look
along the ridge to Helm Crag.

Above: HELM CRAG, LADY AT THE PIANO

Above Grasmere, north-west of the village, a steep fell famous for its distinctive summit rocks dominates the scene. This is Helm Crag, lair of the mountain fox. The curiously shaped crags that have given Helm Crag its notoriety are about 200 yards apart. When viewed from Dunmail Raise the most prominent rock is the Howitzer or Mortar, which is situated at the north-west end of the ridge. At the south-east end, seen from the Swan Hotel, we have the Lion and the Lamb, or as Wordsworth wrote, 'the ancient woman sitting on Helm Crag', known colloquially as 'the old woman playing the organ'. The best views from the summit are over Grasmere.

Left: HELM CRAG, HOWITZER

Victorian tourists gave names to the rocky profiles of Helm Crag, overlooking Grasmere. This summit is a pointing finger at the north-west end of Helm Crag, known as the Howitzer or Mortar.

GRASMERE, WORDSWORTH'S GRAVE

Grasmere today is hardly the tranquil village loved by the poets Wordsworth and De Quincey. Described by Wordsworth as 'the loveliest spot that man hath found', the village of Grasmere lies snugly between the lake and surrounding fells which slope up from its wooded shores.

A simple upright slate slab in the south corner of St Oswald's churchyard marks the resting place of William Wordsworth. His wife Mary and daughter Dora lie buried with him, as well as several other family members. Tradition has it that the origins of the church date back to the seventh century, when Oswald, King of Northumbria, gave his name to an old well here and founded a chapel. Wordsworth himself planted the yew trees in the churchyard.

GRASMERE, RED BANK

This view across Grasmere from Loughrigg Terrace is one of the most popular in the Lake District. It shows the lake in the foreground and the village behind against the backcloth of Helm Crag and Steel Fell. Dorothy Wordsworth wrote in her journal, 'Grasmere looked so beautiful that my heart almost melted away.'

LOUGHRIGG FELL

Although only 1,100 feet high, few mountains give such pleasure as Loughrigg. With its confusion of grassy hummocks and small tarns, it covers a vast acreage between the Rothay and Brathay valleys. The principle summit commands uninterrupted views in all directions and is easily recognised by the Ordnance Survey column next to a small cairn. Low on the side of the fell is the famous path called Loughrigg Terrace, which can easily be reached from the top of Red Bank, a minor road linking Grasmere to the Langdale Valley.

THE BIG CAVE, LOUGHRIGG

Opposite the islands in Rydal Water is a huge cavern, whose entrance can be seen from the far side of the lake. The cave is not natural, but part of an abandoned quarry working. According to Wainwright, 'the whole population of Ambleside could shelter here, although many would be standing in water'.

Above left: **RYDAL WATER**

Constricted between the rocky fell of Nab Scar in the north, and the extensive plateau of Loughrigg Fell in the south, is the smallest of all the lakes. It is known today as Rydal Water, but had previously been called Routhermere or Rothaymere, after the river that flows through it. On leaving the parsonage in Grasmere, Wordsworth went to live in Rydal Mount, a house close to Rydal Water; here, for thirty-seven years, he wrote almost half the poems he published.

Above right: **STEPPING STONES**

After descending from Loughrigg Fell, a pleasant diversion back to Ambleside can be made through the attractive surroundings of Rothay Park by way of the Stepping Stones across the River Rothay at Field Foot.

Right: **STOCKGHYLL CAFÉ, AMBLESIDE**

Time for fish and chips, note the nailed boots.

AFTERWORD

Although the small party did not complete the programme as planned, they did follow it for most of the way. The map used by A.W. for the tour was, I believe, the half inch Bartholomew Tourist and Cycle Map of Westmorland. The close contour lines of this map are at times impossible to follow, and this would explain the discrepancies found in his schedule.

The heights and references are taken from the four OS sheets of 1979 that I used in 1991, and the data is meant only as a guide. These were the last maps to be issued using the old imperial measure. Today's walker with a GPS in his hand will find my figures inaccurate too; this is the extent to which OS mapping has progressed in the 200 years it's been around. I'm not sure that A.W. would have agreed with it; like me, he discovered the landscape by map and compass.

A.W. tells us that the tour would be arduous, but not even he could realise the magnitude of this understatement. The party had no experience of high-level fell walking at all, and their equipment, quite probably moleskin shorts combined with boots or shoes and a poncho or raincoat kept in a Bergen rucksack, matched this. It was a world away from the equipment of today. On day two, after a wet day of ridge walking, they arrived at Calfhow Pike. Across the valley the Saddleback ridge of Blencathra beckoned them, but their schedule told them that they were only halfway through the day and had 10 miles and 10,000 feet of ascent before them. Keswick and a hot meal lay six hours away. We will never know what thoughts passed through their heads when they reached this point; the only one that I had was of despair. To drop to the valley floor and then be confronted by Blencathra was something I didn't want to think about. It was early evening when I reached Threlkeld; the day had been long and hard and relief swept over me as I saw Maggie step from the car.

In 1931 the weather in May was decidedly wet; in fact it was the wettest May since 1925. The monthly totals for precipitation were well above normal for all areas, with the largest of these falls, accompanied by thunderstorms, coming down on the 23rd, 24th and 28th. For A.W. this must have been heartbreaking; it's no surprise when Maudsley tells us that they were forced to retire to Troutbeck on their first day. What he does not say is that this retreat was accompanied by thunder and lightning. The second and third days were no better, and the party again had to change the route, missing out Blencathra and Grasmoor. When they awoke in Buttermere on day four their spirits must have soared; it was a clear day and their only deviation was to miss out Pillar. As they set out from Wasdale on the fifth day they were seeing the fells at their best. Unfortunately it was to be short lived; on the sixth day it turned cloudy once more and the intrepid wanderers must have been pleased that it was their last day.

For whatever reason, A.W. did not keep any notes on this, his 'Grand Tour'. He does not mention it in either of his two autobiographies. We do know that during that week the cloud was of the cumulus or cumulonimbus variety, with its base around 1,000 feet, and at times visibility was just two miles. In these conditions photography would have been almost impossible. Black-and-white film had a rating of twenty-eight ASA in those far-off days of 1931; camera settings were basic and exposures would have been made with the help of a 'Welcome' exposure calculator. Of the photographs taken that week, only three have survived and their locations tell us that they were taken on the good days of Tuesday and Wednesday. It is my belief that the deviations made by the party were due to the weather conditions, and for no other reason; given the right weather, an experienced fell walker could complete this tour in six days. It would be tiring, but, in the words of A.W., well worth the effort.

The eight months that I spent working on 'The Tour' left many memories: snow falling when I reached the first Crinkle on 10 July; an electrical storm whilst on the summit of Cold Pike in August; the exhaustion felt on reaching Threlkeld. My notebook tells me that I ascended Grasmoor eight times within the first fourteen days of June, but it was not until February that I got the shot I wanted. It was events such as these that made the tour what it was: an adventure.

A.W. was admitted to the Kendal Green Hospital on the evening of 7 January 1991; he died at 6p.m. on Sunday, 20 January. It was only then that I thought of all the unasked questions.